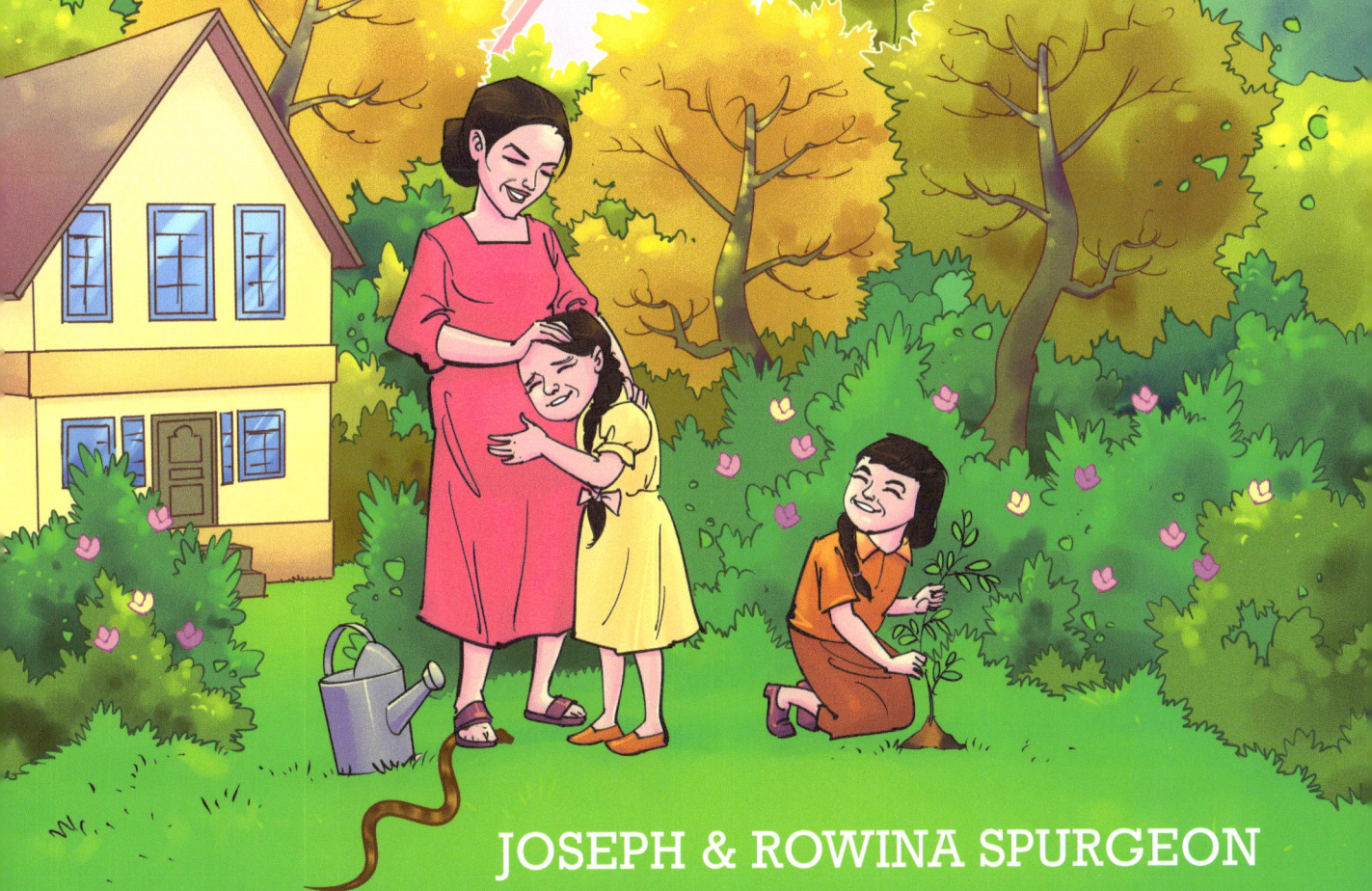

It's GOOD to be a GIRL!

JOSEPH & ROWINA SPURGEON

To Jasmine and Arriana

Published by 5 Solas Press | 5solaspress.com

ISBN: 978-1-7349194-1-7

Dear Dad,

Researchers Betsy Stevenson and Justin Wolfers in a recent report said that "women's life circumstances have improved greatly over the past few decades by most objective measures."[1] Those same researchers also found that since the 1970s, there has been a steady decrease in reported happiness among women. They labeled their report "The Paradox of Declining Female Happiness."[2] Perhaps it is not a paradox at all. Rather what our culture celebrates as progress for women is anything but that.[3] For all the promotion of feminism,[4] the problem is that there has been little talk of promoting the feminine. All discussion of progress solely revolves around the notion that, for women to have value and worth, they must set aside femininity and compete with men. Perhaps when Time's magazine reported in the summer of 2020 that "Women Are Now the Majority of the U.S. Workforce,"[5] this was not a victory but part of the reason that women are less happy.

In the beginning God created male and female and said that it was very good. Man was created first, and woman was created to be his helpmate. Rather than a competition of the sexes, God created a completion of the sexes. God gave Adam a mission to fill and subdue the earth. Eve was made to help him complete that task not by competing in the task nor by trying to take over the work given to him, but rather she was given the awesome responsibility and privilege of giving and nurturing life.[6] God created the man to lead and his wife to submit to his leadership. When, by faith, men and women walk in obedience to the sex God made them, it is good. Femininity is a beautiful creation of God. When women attempt to rebel against it, and since the fall that is their great temptation, nothing is worse.[7]

Therefore, husband, you have a responsibility to love your wives as Christ loves the church. This includes washing her in the word, that is helping her to learn what scripture says about how she is to live. You may not be passive and refuse to lead. Father, you have a great duty to raise up your daughters to be godly women. Do not treat your daughter like one of the boys. Teach her to love and embrace her femininity. Teach her to submit to authority and have a quiet and dignified spirit. Encourage her to love being a helper. It is my hope that this book will be useful for you to raise up daughters who fear the Lord and are praised.[8] It is good to be a girl!

—Joseph Spurgeon

Dear Mom,

Your work that you do for your family is very important and irreplaceable. The Lord has given you a responsibility to train and raise up your girls to become godly women.[9] Soak them in the word of God, the source of all truth, so they may learn and understand the role that God has designed for them.

Our God-given role is to be our husband's helper. Adam was given a task to fill and subdue the earth. Yet God saw that it is not good for a man to be alone.[10] God created Eve to complete Adam by being his helpmate, and enabling him to produce children.[11] Eve was just what he needed–she was suitable for him. She was designed to be a helper, life-giver, nurturer, adorner, and worshiper.

However, Eve listened to that old snake, the devil. She gave into the temptation to think she could be like God. Ever since then, we women have struggled with the desire to rule our husbands rather than help them. But God promised that one of Eve's children would crush the head of that serpent. It was through childbirth, the birth of Jesus (and his death, burial, resurrection), that the snake was defeated. By faith in Christ, we overcome fear, reclaim our God-given role as helper, and reveal that we are daughters of God.[12]

Mom, God is good. Trust Him. Set a good example as a wise woman[13] and encourage your daughters to love the role that God has designed for them. I know it can be hard at times to raise your children, take care of the home, and get everything else done, but remember that the Lord is gracious. There is nobody else on this earth that can provide care like you do. He has created you for a purpose, and he will help you complete it. It's good to be a girl!

—Rowina Spurgeon

---

1. Stevenson, B., & Wolfers, J. (2008). The Paradox of Declining Female Happiness. Retrieved November 10, 2020, from https://law.yale.edu/sites/default/files/documents/pdf/Intellectual_Life/Stevenson_ParadoxDecliningFemaleHappiness_Dec08.pdf
2. Ibid
3. What is often celebrated as progress for women is advancement in birth control, more access to abortion, and more participation in the workforce, lower birth rates, no fault divorce laws, and other ways that women no longer are expected to be homemakers. My wife and I do not believe this to be progress.
4. Feminism is often defined as the belief in social, economic, and political equality of the sexes. This is an attempt to flatten out the distinctions God has hardwired into creation. Both men and women have been made in God's image and are coheirs together in Christ Jesus. But God has established differences between men and women including ordaining that man should lead in the family, church, and state. Feminism is therefore rebellion against God.
5. Law, T. (2020, January 16). Women Are Majority of Workforce, But Still Face Challenges. Retrieved November 10, 2020, from https://time.com/5766787/women-workforce/
6. We acknowledge that not all woman are able to bear children of their own. This is a difficult affliction from the Lord. Many godly women in the bible knew this sorrow. Yet, even the barren woman can be fruitful by her love and care for others. Every woman in the church is to be a mother in the church whether she has children of her own or not.
7. Proverbs 14:1 The wise woman builds her house, But the foolish tears it down with her own hands.
8. Proverbs 31:30
9. Proverbs 6:2
10. Genesis 2:18
11. Genesis 1:28
12. 1 Peter 3:1-6
13. Proverbs 14:1

God Made Women To Be:

Helpers

Genesis 2:18-25, Genesis 24:18-19, Genesis 24:67, 1 Peter 3:1-6, Ecclesiastes 4:9, 1 Corinthians 11:3, Proverbs 18:22, 1 Corinthians 11:8-9, Ephesians 5:22, Matthew 19:4, 1 Corinthians 7:1-40, Proverbs 31:10-12, 1 Timothy 5:14, Proverbs 12:4, Ephesians 5:33, Ephesians 5:23, Ecclesiastes 9:9, 1 Timothy 2:12, Proverbs 5:18, Titus 2:4-5, Proverbs 21:9, Proverbs 25:24, Proverbs 27:15, Genesis 18:1-8

Life-Givers

Genesis 1:28, Genesis 2:24, Genesis 3:15-16, Genesis 3:20, Genesis 4:1-2, Genesis 4:25, Genesis 21:2, Genesis 25:21, Genesis 29:32, Genesis 29:33, Genesis 29:34, Genesis 29:35, Genesis 30:17, Genesis 30:19, Genesis 30:23, 1 Samuel 1, 1 Samuel 2, Matthew 1:20, Luke 1:36, Psalm 127, Psalm 128, Exodus 1:17, Exodus 21:22, Judges 13:3, Ruth 4:13, Psalm 22:10, Isaiah 26:17, Luke 2:7, John 16:21, 1 Corinthians 11:12, 1 Timothy 2:15, Genesis 24:60, Titus 2:4, Psalm 113:9

Nurturers

1 Kings 3:16-27, Proverbs 31:10-31, 1 Timothy 5:14, Proverbs 31:1, Ezekiel 16:49, Titus 2:3-5, Acts 7:20-21, Exodus 2:5-10, Proverbs 22:6, Proverbs 19:18, Psalm 22:9, Isaiah 66:10-22, Luke 11:27-28, Luke 10:38-42, Ruth 1:14, Ruth 2:11, 1 Samuel 2:19, Psalm 131:2, Proverbs 1:8, Proverbs 6:20, Proverbs 29:15, Isaiah 66:13, Galatians 4:26, 1 Thessalonians 2:7, Acts 9:36, 1 Kings 1:3-4

Adorners

Genesis 3:7, 1 Timothy 2:9-14, 1 Corinthians 11:1-16. 1 Peter 3: 1-6, Genesis 24:16, Genesis 24:64-65, Genesis 29:17, Proverbs 31: 22, Proverbs 31:25, Song of Solomon 1:13, Song of Solomon 7:7, Ruth 3:3, Proverbs 11:22, Revelation 21:2, Deuteronomy 22:5, Prov 6:25, Prov 23:27, 1 Samuel 25:3, Song of Solomon 4:7, Song of Songs 1:15-16, Proverbs 11:16, . Esther 2:7, Genesis 12:11, Genesis 12:14, Genesis 26:7, Matthew 23:27, Psalm 45:13

Worshippers

1 Samuel 2:1-10, Proverbs 23:25, Luke 1:46-55, 1 Corinthians 11:1-16, 1 Corinthians 14:34-35, Judges 5, Acts 1:14, Psalm 48:11, Jeremiah 9:20, Zephaniah 3:14, Zechariah 2:10, Zechariah 9:9, Luke 2:36-38, Luke 7:36-50, Exodus 15:20-21, 2 Samuel 19:35, 2 Chronicles 35:25, Psalm 68:25, Ephesians 5:19, John 4:21

His Daughters

Genesis 1:27, Genesis 1:31, Genesis 3:15, 1 Peter 3:7, Ephesians 5:1, Romans 16:3, Romans 16:3, 2 Timothy 1:5, Galatians 3:28, Exodus 20:12, Exodus 21:15, Exodus 21:17, Leviticus 19:3, Deuteronomy 5:16, Deuteronomy 27:16, Ruth 3:11, 2 Chronicles 31:18, Job 42:15, Psalm 45:10-12, Psalm 144:12, Proverbs 31:29, Isaiah 62:11, Matthew 9:22, 2 Corinthians 6:18

"Let our sons in their youth be as grown-up plants, And our daughters as corner pillars fashioned as for a palace."

Psalm 144:12

Hi! I'm Jasmine. That's my sister, Arriana, helping Momma with the laundry. Say hi, Sis!

Wow, what a wonderful day God has made!
Do you know what else God made? He made little
girls like my sister and me. It's good to be a girl.

Why is it good to be a girl?
Well, let me tell you.

It's good to be a girl because God
made girls to be helpers.

Daddy is Momma's husband, and Momma is his wife.
Daddy loves Momma and takes care of all of us.

Momma loves Daddy and likes helping him. He's the leader of our family, and we all obey him. One day I will be a helper to my husband the way Momma is to Daddy.

It's good to be a girl because God made girls to be life-givers.

Momma is pregnant, which means she has a
new baby growing in her belly. Only women
can have babies. Daddy says it's one of
the ways God made women special.

We're so excited to meet our new baby brother. Arriana and I practice taking care of a real baby by taking good care of our dolls.

It's good to be a girl because God made girls to be nurturers. What is a nurturer?

A nurturer is someone who takes care of
someone else. Momma always looks out for us.

Momma always knows what to do
when we get sick or hurt.

It's good to be a girl because God
made girls to be adorners.
To adorn something is to make it pretty.

Daddy says God gave girls long hair to make them glorious. He always tells us we look pretty when we are getting ready for church.

Momma is always respectful and polite. God thinks a gentle and quiet spirit is beautiful, and God wants us to care more about honoring others than about trying to get attention for ourselves.

It's good to be a girl because God
made girls to be worshippers.

O Worship the King ...

It's good to worship God.

It's good to be a girl because God
made girls to be His daughters.

Because we believe Jesus died on the cross and rose again, we can talk to God anytime.

Because God has been so good to us, our family loves to share the truth about God. Daddy does the talking, and we do the praying. We are a good team.

I am so thankful that God made me because….

It's good to be a girl.

www.ingramcontent.com/pod-product-compliance
Lightning Source LLC
Chambersburg PA
CBHW042015090426
42811CB00015B/1650